PROSERPINE
&
MIDAS

Two unpublished Mythological Dramas
by
MARY SHELLEY

Edited with Introduction
by
A. KOSZUL

PREFATORY NOTE.

The editor came across the unpublished texts included in this volume as early as 1905. Perhaps he ought to apologize for delaying their appearance in print. The fact is he has long been afraid of overrating their intrinsic value. But as the great Shelley centenary year has come, perhaps this little monument of his wife's collaboration may take its modest place among the tributes which will be paid to his memory. For Mary Shelley's mythological dramas can at least claim to be the proper setting for some of the most beautiful lyrics of the poet, which so far have been read in undue isolation. And even as a literary sign of those times, as an example of that classical renaissance which the romantic period fostered, they may not be altogether negligible.

These biographical and literary points have been dealt with in an introduction for which the kindest help was long ago received from the late Dr. Garnett and the late Lord Abinger. Sir Walter Raleigh was also among the first to give both encouragement and guidance. My friends M. Emile Pons and Mr. Roger Ingpen have read the book in manuscript. The authorities of the Bodleian Library and of the Clarendon Press have been as generously helpful as is their well-known wont. To all the editor wishes to record his acknowledgements and thanks.

STRASBOURG.

INTRODUCTION.

I.

'The compositions published in Mrs. Shelley's lifetime afford but an inadequate conception of the intense sensibility and mental vigour of this extraordinary woman.'

Thus wrote Dr. Garnett, in 1862 (Preface to his Relics of Shelley). The words of praise may have sounded unexpectedly warm at that date. Perhaps the present volume will make the reader more willing to subscribe, or less inclined to demur.

Mary Godwin in her younger days certainly possessed a fair share of that nimbleness of invention which generally characterizes women of letters. Her favourite pastime as a child, she herself testifies,[1] had been to write stories. And a dearer pleasure had been—to use her own characteristic abstract and elongated way of putting it—'the following up trains of thought which had for their subject the formation of a succession of imaginary incidents'. All readers of Shelley's life remember how later on, as a girl of nineteen—and a two years' wife—she was present, 'a devout but nearly silent listener', at the long symposia held by her husband and Byron in Switzerland (June 1816), and how the pondering over 'German horrors', and a common resolve to perpetrate ghost stories of their own, led her to imagine that most unwomanly of all feminine romances, Frankenstein. The paradoxical effort was paradoxically successful, and, as publishers' lists aver to this day, Frankenstein's monster has turned out to be the hardest-lived specimen of the 'raw-head-and-bloody-bones' school of romantic tales. So much, no doubt, to the credit of Mary Shelley. But more creditable, surely, is the fact that she was not tempted, as 'Monk' Lewis had been, to persevere in those lugubrious themes.

Although her publishers—et pour cause—insisted on styling her 'the author of Frankenstein', an entirely different vein appears in her later productions. Indeed, a quiet reserve of tone, a slow, sober, and sedate bearing, are henceforth characteristic of all her literary attitudes. It is almost a case of running from one to the other extreme. The force of style which even adverse critics acknowledged in Frankenstein was sometimes perilously akin to the most disputable kinds of romantic rant. But in the historical or society novels which followed, in the contributions which graced the 'Keepsakes' of the thirties, and even —alas—in the various prefaces and commentaries which accompanied the publication of so many poems of Shelley, his wife succumbed to an increasing habit of almost Victorian reticence and dignity. And those later novels and tales, though they sold well in their days and were kindly reviewed, can hardly boast of any reputation now. Most of them are pervaded by a brooding spirit of melancholy of the 'moping' rather than the 'musical' sort, and consequently rather ineffective as an artistic motive. Students of Shelley occasionally scan those pages with a view to pick some obscure 'hints and indirections', some veiled reminiscences, in the stories of the adventures and misfortunes of The Last Man or Lodore. And the books may be good biography at times—they are never life.

Altogether there is a curious contrast between the two aspects, hitherto revealed, of Mary Shelley's literary activities. It is as if the pulse which had been beating so wildly, so frantically, in Frankenstein (1818), had lapsed, with Valperga (1823) and the rest, into an increasingly sluggish flow.

The following pages may be held to bridge the gap between those two extremes in a felicitous way. A more purely artistic mood, instinct with the serene joy and clear warmth of Italian skies, combining a good deal of youthful buoyancy with a sort of quiet and unpretending philosophy, is here represented. And it is submitted that the little classical fancies which Mrs. Shelley never ventured to publish are quite as worthy of consideration as her more ambitious prose works.

For one thing they give us the longest poetical effort of the writer. The moon of Epipsychidion never seems to have been thrilled with the music of the highest spheres. Yet there were times when Shelley's inspiration and example fired her into something more than her usual calm and cold brilliancy.

One of those periods—perhaps the happiest period in Mary's life— was during the early months in Italy of the English 'exiles'. 'She never was more strongly impelled to write than at this time; she felt her powers fresh and strong within her; all she wanted was some motive, some suggestion to guide her in the choice of a subject.'[2]

Shelley then expected her to try her hand at a drama, perhaps on the terrible story of the Cenci, or again on the catastrophes of Charles the First. Her Frankenstein was attracting more attention than had ever been granted to his own works. And Shelley, with that touching simplicity which characterized his loving moments, showed the greatest confidence in the literary career of his wife. He helped her and encouraged her in every way. He then translated for her Plato's Symposium. He led her on in her Latin and Italian studies. He wanted her—probably as a sort of preliminary exercise before her flight into tragedy—to translate Alfieri's Myrrha. 'Remember Charles the First, and do you be prepared to bring at least some of Myrrha translated,' he wrote; 'remember, remember Charles the First and Myrrha,' he insisted; and he quoted, for her benefit, the presumptuous aphorism of Godwin, in St. Leon, 'There is nothing which the human mind can conceive which it may not execute'.[3]

But in the year that followed these auspicious days, the strain and stress of her life proved more powerful on Mary Shelley than the inspiration of literature. The loss of her little girl Clara, at Venice, on the 24th of September 1818, was cruel enough. However, she tried hard not to show the 'pusillanimous disposition' which, Godwin assured his daughter, characterizes the persons 'that sink long under a calamity of this nature'.[4] But the death of her boy, William, at Rome, on the 4th of June 1819, reduced her to a 'kind of despair'. Whatever it could be to her husband, Italy no longer was for her a 'paradise of exiles'. The flush and excitement of the early months, the 'first fine careless rapture', were for ever gone. 'I shall never recover that blow,' Mary wrote on the 27th of June 1819; 'the thought never leaves me for a single moment; everything on earth has lost its interest for me,' This time her imperturbable father 'philosophized' in vain. With a more sympathetic and acuter intelligence of her case, Leigh Hunt insisted (July 1819) that she should try and give her paralysing sorrow some literary expression, 'strike her pen into some... genial subject... and bring up a fountain of gentle tears for us'. But the poor childless mother could only rehearse her complaint—'to have won, and thus cruelly to have lost' (4 August 1819). In fact she had, on William's death, discontinued her diary.

Yet on the date just mentioned, as Shelley reached his twenty-seven years, she plucked up courage and resumed the task. Shelley, however absorbed by the creative ardour of his Annus mirabilis, could not but observe that his wife's 'spirits continued wretchedly depressed' (5 August 1819); and though masculine enough to resent the fact at times more than pity it, he was human enough to persevere in that habit of co-operative reading and writing which is one of the finest traits of his married life. 'I write in the morning,' his wife testifies, 'read Latin till 2, when we dine; then I read some English book, and two cantos of Dante with Shelley'[5] —a fair average, no doubt, of the homely aspect of the great days which produced The Cenci and Prometheus.

On the 12th November, in Florence, the birth of a second son, Percy Florence Shelley, helped Mary out of her sense of bereavement. Subsequent letters still occasionally admit 'low spirits'. But the entries in the Journal make it clear that the year 1819-20 was one of the most pleasantly industrious of her life. Not Dante only, but a motley series of books, great and small, ancient and modern, English and foreign, bespoke her attention. Not content with Latin, and the extemporized translations which Shelley could give her of Plato's Republic, she started Greek in 1820, and soon came to delight in it. And again she thought of original composition. 'Write', 'work,' — the words now occur daily in her Journal. These must mainly refer to the long historical novel, which she had planned, as early as 1819,[6] under the title of Castruccio, Prince of Lucca, and which was not published until 1823, as Valperga. It was indeed a laborious task. The novel 'illustrative of the manners of the Middle Ages in Italy' had to be 'raked out of fifty old books', as Shelley said. [7]

But heavy as the undertaking must have been, it certainly did not engross all the activities of Shelley's wife in this period. And it seems highly probable that the two little mythological dramas which we here publish belong to this same year 1820.

The evidence for this date is as follows. Shelley's lyrics, which these dramas include, were published by his wife (Posthumous Poems, 1824) among the 'poems written in 1820'. Another composition, in blank verse, curiously similar to Mary's own work, entitled Orpheus, has been allotted by Dr. Garnett (Relics of Shelley, 1862) to the same category. 8 Again, it may well be more than a coincidence, that the Proserpine motive occurs in that passage from Dante's Purgatorio, canto 28, on 'Matilda gathering flowers', which Shelley is known to have translated shortly before Medwin's visit in the late autumn of 1820.

    O come, that I may hear
Thy song: like Proserpine, in Enna's glen,
Thou seemest to my fancy,—singing here,
And gathering flowers, as that fair maiden, when
She lost the spring and Ceres her more dear.9

But we have a far more important, because a direct, testimony in a manuscript addition made by Thomas Medwin in the margin of a copy of his Life of Shelley (1847). 10 The passage is clearly intended—though chronology is no more than any other exact science the 'forte' of that most tantalizing of biographers—to refer to the year 1820.

'Mrs. Shelley had at this time been writing some little Dramas on classical subjects, one of which was the Rape of Proserpine, a very graceful composition which she has never published. Shelley contributed to this the exquisite fable of Arethusa and the Invocation to Ceres.—Among the Nymphs gathering flowers on Enna were two whom she called Ino and Uno, names which I remember in the Dialogue were irresistibly ludicrous. She also wrote one on Midas, into which were introduced by Shelley, in the Contest between Pan and Apollo, the Sublime Effusion of the latter, and Pan's characterised Ode.'

This statement of Medwin finally settles the question. The 'friend' at whose request, Mrs. Shelley says, 11 the lyrics were written by her husband, was herself. And she was the author of the dramas.12

The manuscript (Bodleian Library, MS. Shelley, d. 2) looks like a cheap exercise-book, originally of 40, now of 36 leaves, 8 1/4 x 6 inches, in boards. The contents are the dramas here presented, written in a clear legible hand—the equable hand of Mrs. Shelley. 13

There are very few words corrected or cancelled. It is obviously a fair copy. Mr. C. D. Locock, in his Examination of the Shelley Manuscripts in the Bodleian Library (Clarendon Press, Oxford, 1903, pp. 24-25), has already pointed out the valuable emendations of the 'received' text of Shelley's lyrics which are found here. In fact the only mystery is why neither Shelley, nor Mary in the course of her long widowed years, should have published these curious, and surely not contemptible, by-products of their co-operation in the fruitful year 1820.

Footnotes

1 Preface to the 1831 edition of Frankenstein.
2 Mrs. Marshall, The Life and Letters of Mary W. Shelley, i. 216.
3 Letter from Padua, 22 September 1818.
4 27 October 1818
5 Letter to Mrs. Hunt, 28 August 1819.
6 She had 'thought of it' at Marlow, as appears from her letter to Mrs. Gisborne, 30 June 1821 (in Mrs. Marshall, i. p. 291); but the materials for it were not found before the stay at Naples, and it was not actually begun 'till a year afterwards, at Pisa' (ibid.).
7 Letter to T. L. Peacock, November 1820.
8 Dr. Garnett, in his prefatory note, states that Orpheus 'exists only in a transcript by Mrs. Shelley, who has written in playful allusion to her toils as amanuensis Aspetto fin che il diluvio cala, ed allora cerco di posare argine alle sue parole'. The poem is thus supposed to have been Shelley's attempt at improvisation, if not indeed a translation from the Italian of the 'improvvisatore' Sgricci. The Shelleys do not seem to have come to know and hear Sgricci before the end of December 1820. The Italian note after all has no very clear import. And Dr. Garnett in 1905 inclined to the view that Orpheus was the work not of Shelley, but of his wife. A comparison of that fragment and the dramas here published seems to me to suggest the same conclusion, though in both cases Mary Shelley must have been helped by her husband.
9 As published by Medwin, 1834 and 1847.
10 The copy, 2 vols., was sold at Sotheby's on the 6th December 1906: Mr. H. Buxton Forman (who was, I think, the buyer) published

the contents in The Life of Percy Bysshe Shelley, By Thomas Medwin, A New Edition printed from a copy copiously amended and extended by the Author . . . Milford, 1913. The passage here quoted appears on p. 27 of the 2nd vol. of the 1847 edition (Forman ed., p. 252)

11 The Hymns of Pan and Apollo were first published by Mrs. Shelley in the Posthumous Poems, 1824, with a note saying that they had been 'written at the request of a friend to be inserted in a drama on the subject of Midas'. Arethusa appeared in the same volume, dated 'Pisa, 1820'. Proserpine's song was not published before the first collected edition of 1839.

12 Not E. E. Williams (Buxton Forman, ed. 1882, vol. iv, p. 34). The manuscript of the poetical play composed about 1822 by the latter, 'The Promise', with Shelley's autograph poem ('Night! with all thine eyes look down'), was given to the Bodleian Library in 1914.

13 Shelley's lyrics are also in his wife's writing—Mr. Locock is surely mistaken in assuming two different hands to this manuscript (The Poems of Percy Bysshe Shelley, Methuen, 1909, vol. iii, p. xix).

II.

For indeed there is more than a personal interest attached to these writings of Mrs. Shelley's. The fact that the same mind which had revelled, a few years earlier, in the fantastical horrors of Frankenstein's abortive creation, could now dwell on the melancholy fate of Proserpine or the humorous disappointment of Midas, and delight in their subtle poetical or moral symbolism—this fact has its significance. It is one of the earliest indications of the revival, in the heart of Romanticism, of the old love of classical myths and classical beauty.

The subject is a wide one, and cannot be adequately dealt with in this place. But a few words may not be superfluous for a correct historical appreciation of Mrs. Shelley's attempt.

How deficient had been the sense of classical beauty in the so-called classical age of English literature, is a trite consideration of criticism. The treatment of mythology is particularly conclusive on this point. Throughout the 'Augustan' era, mythology was approached as a mere treasure-house of pleasant fancies, artificial decorations, 'motives', whether sumptuous or meretricious. Allusions to Jove and Venus, Mercury, Apollo, or Bacchus, are of course found in every other page of Dryden, Pope, Prior, Swift, Gay, and Parnell. But no fresh presentation, no loving interpretation, of the old myths occur anywhere. The immortal stories were then part and parcel of a sort of poetical curriculum through which the whole school must be taken by the stern masters Tradition and Propriety. There is little to be wondered at, if this matter of curriculum was treated by the more passive scholars as a matter of course, and by the sharper and less reverent disciples as a matter of fun. Indeed, if any personality is then evinced in the adaptation of these old world themes, it is generally connected with a more or less emphatic disparagement or grotesque distortion of their real meaning.

When Dryden, for example, makes use of the legend of Midas, in his Wife of Bath's Tale, he makes, not Midas's minister, but his queen, tell the mighty secret—and thus secures another hit at woman's loquacity.

Prior's Female Phaëton is a younger sister, who, jealous of her elder's success, thus pleads with her 'mamma':

I'll have my earl as well as she
  Or know the reason why.

And she wants to flaunt it accordingly.

Finally,

Fondness prevailed; mamma gave way;
  Kitty, at heart's desire,
Obtained the chariot for a day,
  And set the world on fire.

Pandora, in Parnell's Hesiod or the Rise of Woman, is only a

> 'shining vengeance...
A pleasing bosom-cheat, a specious ill'

sent by the gods upon earth to punish the race of Prometheus.

The most poetical fables of Greece are desecrated by Gay into mere miniatures for the decoration of his Fan.

Similar instances abound later on. When Armstrong brings in an apostrophe to the Naiads, it is in the course of a Poetical Essay on the Art of Preserving Health. And again, when Cowper stirs himself to intone an Ode to Apollo, it is in the same mock-heroic vein:

Patron of all those luckless brains,
  That to the wrong side leaning
Indite much metre with much pains
  And little or no meaning...

Even in Gray's—'Pindaric Gray's'—treatment of classical themes, there is a sort of pervading ennui, or the forced appreciativeness of a gouty, disappointed man. The daughter of Jove to whom he dedicates his hymns too often is 'Adversity'. And classical reminiscences have, even with him, a dull musty tinge which recalls the antiquarian in his Cambridge college-rooms rather than the visitor to Florence and Rome. For one thing, his allusions are too many, and too transitory, to appear anything but artistic tricks and verse-making tools. The 'Aegean deep', and 'Delphi's steep', and 'Meander's amber waves', and the 'rosy-crowned Loves', are too cursorily summoned, and dismissed, to suggest that they have been brought in for their own sweet sakes.

It was thus with all the fine quintessences of ancient lore, with all the pearl-like accretions of the faiths and fancies of the old world: they were handled about freely as a kind of curious but not so very rare coins, which found no currency in the deeper thoughts of our modern humanity, and could therefore be used as a mere badge of the learning and taste of a literary 'coterie'.

The very names of the ancient gods and heroes were in fact assuming that abstract anaemic look which common nouns have in everyday language. Thus, when Garrick, in his verses Upon a Lady's Embroidery, mentions 'Arachne', it is obvious that he does not expect the reader to think of the daring challenger of Minerva's art, or the Princess of Lydia, but just of a plain spider. And again, when Falconer, in his early Monody on the death of the Prince of Wales, expresses a rhetorical wish

'to aid hoarse howling Boreas with his sighs,'

that particular son of Astræus, whose love for the nymph Orithyia was long unsuccessful, because he could not 'sigh', is surely far from the poet's mind; and 'to swell the wind', or 'the gale', would have served his turn quite as well, though less 'elegantly'.

Even Gibbon, with all his partiality for whatever was pre- or post-Christian, had indeed no better word than 'elegant' for the ancient mythologies of Greece and Rome, and he surely reflected no particularly advanced opinion when he praised and damned, in one breath, 'the pleasant and absurd system of Paganism.'[1] No wonder if in his days, and for a long time after, the passionate giants of the Ages of Fable had dwindled down to the pretty puppets with which the daughters of the gentry had to while away many a school hour.

But the days of this rhetorical—or satirical, didactic—or perfunctory, treatment of classical themes were doomed. It is the glory of Romanticism to have opened 'magic casements' not only on 'the foam of perilous seas' in the West, but also on

    the chambers of the East,
The chambers of the Sun, that now
  From ancient melody had ceased.[2]

Romanticism, as a freshening up of all the sources of life, a general rejuvenescence of the soul, a ubiquitous visiting of the spirit of delight and wonder, could not confine itself to the fields of mediaeval romance. Even the records of the Greek and Roman thought assumed a new beauty; the classical sense was let free from its antiquarian trammels, and the perennial fanes resounded to the songs of a more impassioned worship.

The change, however, took some time. And it must be admitted that in England, especially, the Romantic movement was slow to go back to classical themes. Winckelmann and Goethe, and Chénier—the last, indeed, practically all unknown to his contemporaries—had long rediscovered Antiquity, and felt its pulse anew, and praised its enduring power, when English poetry had little, if anything, to show in answer to the plaintive invocation of Blake to the Ancient Muses.

The first generation of English Romantics either shunned the subject altogether, or simply echoed Blake's isolated lines in isolated passages as regretful and almost as despondent. From Persia to Paraguay Southey could wander and seek after exotic themes; his days could be 'passed among the dead'—but neither the classic lands nor the classic heroes ever seem to have detained him. Walter Scott's 'sphere of sensation may be almost exactly limited by the growth of heather', as Ruskin says;[3] and when he came to Rome, his last illness prevented him from any attempt he might have wished to make to enlarge his field of vision. Wordsworth was even less far-travelled, and his home-made poetry never thought of the 'Pagan' and his 'creed outworn', but as a distinct pis-aller in the way of inspiration.[4] And again, though Coleridge has a few magnificent lines about them, he seems to have even less willingly than Wordsworth hearkened after

The intelligible forms of ancient poets,
The fair humanities of old religion.[5]

It was to be otherwise with the later English Romantic poets. They lived and worked at a time when the whole atmosphere and even the paraphernalia of literary composition had just undergone a considerable change. After a period of comparative seclusion and self-concentration, England at the Peace of Amiens once more found its way to Europe—and vice versa. And from our point of view this widening of prospects is especially noticeable. For the classical revival in Romanticism appears to be closely connected with it.

It is an alluring subject to investigate. How the progress of scholarship, the recent 'finds' of archaeology, the extension of travelling along Mediterranean shores, the political enthusiasms evoked by the stirrings of young Italy and young Greece, all combined to reawaken in the poetical imagination of the times the dormant memories of antiquity has not yet been told by the historians of literature.[6]

But—and this is sufficient for our purpose—every one knows what the Elgin Marbles have done for Keats and Shelley; and what inspirations were derived from their pilgrimages in classic lands by all the poets of this and the following generation, from Byron to Landor. Such experiences could not but react on the common conception of mythology. A knowledge of the great classical sculpture of Greece could not but invest with a new dignity and chastity the notions which so far had been nurtured on the Venus de' Medici and the Belvedere Apollo—even Shelley lived and possibly died under their spell. And 'returning to the nature which had inspired the ancient myths', the Romantic poets must have felt with a keener sense 'their exquisite vitality'.[7] The whole tenor of English Romanticism may be said to have been affected thereby.

For English Romanticism—and this is one of its most distinctive merits—had no exclusiveness about it. It was too spontaneous, one would almost say, too unconscious, ever to be clannish. It grew, untrammelled by codes, uncrystallized into formulas, a living thing always, not a subject-matter for grandiloquent manifestoes and more or less dignified squabbles. It could therefore absorb and turn to account elements which seemed antagonistic to it in the more sophisticated forms it assumed in other literatures. Thus, whilst French Romanticism—in spite of what it may or may not have owed to Chénier—became often distinctly, deliberately, wilfully anti-classical, whilst for example[8] Victor Hugo in that all-comprehending Légende des Siècles could find room for the Hegira and for Zim-Zizimi, but did not consecrate a single line to the departed glories of mythical Greece, the Romantic poets of England may claim to have restored in freshness and purity the religion of antiquity. Indeed their voice was so convincing that even the great Christian chorus that broke out afresh in the Victorian era could not entirely drown it, and Elizabeth Barrett had an apologetic way of dismissing 'the dead Pan', and all the 'vain false gods of Hellas', with an acknowledgement of

> your beauty which confesses
> Some chief Beauty conquering you.

This may be taken to have been the average attitude, in the forties, towards classical mythology. That twenty years before, at least in the Shelley circle, it was far less grudging, we now have definite proof.

Not only was Shelley prepared to admit, with the liberal opinion of the time, that ancient mythology 'was a system of nature concealed under the veil of allegory', a system in which 'a thousand fanciful fables contained a secret and mystic meaning':[9] he was prepared to go a considerable step farther, and claim that there was no essential difference between ancient mythology and the theology of the Christians, that both were interpretations, in more or less figurative language, of the great mysteries of being, and indeed that the earlier interpretation, precisely because it was more frankly figurative and poetical than the later one, was better fitted to stimulate and to allay the sense of wonder which ought to accompany a reverent and high-souled man throughout his life-career.

In the earlier phase of Shelley's thought, this identification of the ancient and the modern faiths was derogatory to both. The letter which he had written in 1812 for ihe edification of Lord Ellenborough revelled in the contemplation of a time 'when the Christian religion shall have faded from the earth, when its memory like that of Polytheism now shall remain, but remain only as the subject of ridicule and wonder'. But as time went on, Shelley's views became less purely negative. Instead of ruling the adversaries back to back out of court, he bethought himself of venturing a plea in favour of the older and weaker one. It may have been in 1817 that he contemplated an 'Essay in favour of polytheism'.[10] He was then living on the fringe of a charmed circle of amateur and adventurous Hellenists who could have furthered the scheme. His great friend, Thomas Love Peacock, 'Greeky Peaky', was a personal acquaintance of Thomas Taylor 'the Platonist', alias 'Pagan Taylor'. And Taylor's translations and commentaries of Plato had been favourites of Shelley in his college days. Something at least of Taylor's queer mixture of flaming enthusiasm and tortuous ingenuity may be said to appear in the unexpected document we have now to examine.

It is a little draft of an Essay, which occurs, in Mrs. Shelley's handwriting, as an insertion in her Journal for the Italian period. The fragment—for it is no more—must be quoted in full.[11]

The necessity of a Belief in the
Heathen Mythology
to a Christian

If two facts are related not contradictory of equal probability & with equal evidence, if we believe one we must believe the other.

1st. There is as good proof of the Heathen Mythology as of the Christian Religion.

2ly. that they [do] not contradict one another.

Con[clusion]. If a man believes in one he must believe in both.

Examination of the proofs of the Xtian religion—the Bible & its authors. The twelve stones that existed in the time of the writer prove the miraculous passage of the river Jordan.[12] The immoveability of the Island of Delos proves the accouchement of Latona[13] —the Bible of the Greek religion consists in Homer, Hesiod & the Fragments of Orpheus &c.—All that came afterwards to be considered apocryphal—Ovid = Josephus—of each of these writers we may believe just what we cho[o]se.

To seek in these Poets for the creed & proofs of mythology which are as follows—Examination of these—1st with regard to proof—2 in contradiction or conformity to the Bible—various apparitions of God in that Book [—] Jupiter considered by himself—his attributes —disposition [—] acts—whether as God revealed himself as the

Almighty to the Patriarchs & as Jehovah to the Jews he did not reveal himself as Jupiter to the Greeks—the possibility of various revelations—that he revealed himself to Cyrus.14

The inferior deities—the sons of God & the Angels—the difficulty of Jupiter's children explained away—the imagination of the poets—of the prophets—whether the circumstance of the sons of God living with women15 being related in one sentence makes it more probable than the details of Greek—Various messages of the Angels—of the deities—Abraham, Lot or Tobit. Raphael [—]Mercury to Priam16 — Calypso & Ulysses—the angel w^d then play the better part of the two whereas he now plays the worse. The ass of Balaam—Oracles—Prophets. The revelation of God as Jupiter to the Greeks—-a more successful revelation than that as Jehovah to the Jews—Power, wisdom, beauty, & obedience of the Greeks—greater & of longer continuance—than those of the Jews. Jehovah's promises worse kept than Jupiter's—the Jews or Prophets had not a more consistent or decided notion concerning after life & the Judgements of God than the Greeks [—] Angels disappear at one time in the Bible & afterwards appear again. The revelation to the Greeks more complete than to the Jews—prophesies of Christ by the heathens more incontrovertible than those of the Jews. The coming of X. a confirmation of both religions. The cessation of oracles a proof of this. The Xtians better off than any but the Jews as blind as the Heathens—Much more conformable to an idea of [the] goodness of God that he should have revealed himself to the Greeks than that he left them in ignorance. Vergil & Ovid not truth of the heathen Mythology, but the interpretation of a heathen—as Milton's Paradise Lost is the interpretation of a Christian religion of the Bible. The interpretation of the mythology of Vergil & the interpretation of the Bible by Milton compared—whether one is more inconsistent than the other—In what they are contradictory. Prometheus desmotes quoted by Paul17 [—] all religion false except that which is revealed —revelation depends upon a certain degree of civilization—writing necessary—no oral tradition to be a part of faith—the worship of the Sun no revelation—Having lost the books [of] the Egyptians we have no knowledge of their peculiar revelations. If the revelation of God to the Jews on Mt Sinai had been more peculiar & impressive than some of those to the Greeks they w^d not immediately after have worshiped a calf—A latitude in revelation—How to judge of prophets—the proof [of] the Jewish Prophets being prophets.

The only public revelation that Jehovah ever made of himself was on Mt Sinai—Every other depended upon the testimony of a very few & usually of a single individual—We will first therefore consider the revelation of Mount Sinai. Taking the fact plainly it happened thus. The Jews were told by a man whom they believed to have supernatural powers that they were to prepare for that God w^d reveal himself in three days on the mountain at the sound of a trumpet. On the 3rd day there was a cloud & lightning on the mountain & the voice of a trumpet extremely loud. The people were ordered to stand round the foot of the mountain & not on pain of death to infringe upon the bounds—The man in whom they confided went up the mountain & came down again bringing them word

The draft unfortunately leaves off here, and we are unable to know for certain whether this Shelleyan paradox, greatly daring, meant to minimize the importance of the 'only public revelation' granted to the chosen people. But we have enough to understand the general trend of the argument. It did not actually intend to sap the foundations of Scriptural authority. But it was bold enough to risk a little shaking in order to prove that the Sacred Books of the Greeks and Romans did not, after all, present us with a much more rickety structure. This was a task of conciliation rather than destruction. And yet even this conservative view of the Shelleys' exegesis cannot—and will not—detract from the value of the above document. Surely, this curious theory of the equal 'inspiration' of Polytheism and the Jewish or Christian religions, whether it was invented or simply espoused by Mrs. Shelley, evinces in her—for the time being at least—a very considerable share of that adventurous if somewhat uncritical alacrity of mind which carried the poet through so many religious and political problems. It certainly vindicates her, more completely perhaps than anything hitherto published, against the strictures of those who knew her chiefly or exclusively in later years, and could speak of her as a 'most conventional slave', who 'even affected the pious dodge', and 'was not a suitable companion for the poet'.[18] Mrs. Shelley—at twenty-three years of age—had not yet run the full 'career of her humour'; and her enthusiasm for classical mythology may well have, later on, gone the way of her admiration for Spinoza, whom she read with Shelley that winter (1820-1), as Medwin notes,[19] and 'whose arguments she then thought irrefutable —tempora mutantur!'

However that may be, the two little mythological dramas on Proserpine and Midas assume, in the light of that enthusiasm, a special interest. They stand—or fall—both as a literary, and to a certain extent as an intellectual effort. They are more than an attitude, and not much less than an avowal. Not only do they claim our attention as the single poetical work of any length which seems to have been undertaken by Mrs. Shelley; they are a unique and touching monument of that intimate co-operation which at times, especially in the early years in Italy, could make the union of 'the May' and 'the Elf' almost unreservedly delightful. It would undoubtedly be fatuous exaggeration to ascribe a very high place in literature to these little Ovidian fancies of Mrs. Shelley. The scenes, after all, are little better than adaptations—fairly close adaptations— of the Latin poet's well-known tales.

Even Proserpine, though clearly the more successful of the two, both more strongly knit as drama, and less uneven in style and versification, cannot for a moment compare with the far more original interpretations of Tennyson, Swinburne, or Meredith.[20] But it is hardly fair to draw in the great names of the latter part of the century. The parallel would be more illuminating—and the final award passed on Mrs. Shelley's attempt more favourable—if we were to think of a contemporary production like 'Barry Cornwall's' Rape of Proserpine, which, being published in 1820, it is just possible that the Shelleys should have known. B. W. Procter's poem is also a dramatic 'scene', written 'in imitation of the mode originated by the Greek Tragic Writers'. In fact those hallowed models seem to have left far fewer traces in Barry Cornwall's verse than the Alexandrian—or pseudo-Alexandrian—tradition of meretricious graces and coquettish fancies, which the eighteenth century had already run to death.[21] And, more damnable still, the poetical essence of the legend, the identification of Proserpine's twofold existence with the grand alternation of nature's seasons, has been entirely neglected by the author. Surely his work, though published, is quite as deservedly obscure as Mrs. Shelley's derelict manuscript. Midas has the privilege, if it be one, of not challenging any obvious comparison. The subject, since Lyly's and Dryden's days, has hardly attracted the attention of the poets. It was so eminently fit for the lighter kinds of presentation that the agile bibliographer who aimed at completeness would have to go through a fairly long list of masques,[22] comic operas, or 'burlettas', all dealing with the ludicrous misfortunes of the Phrygian king. But an examination of these would be sheer pedantry in this place. Here again Mrs. Shelley has stuck to her Latin source as closely as she could.[23] She has made a gallant attempt to connect the two stories with which Midas has ever since Ovid's days been associated, and a distinct—indeed a too perceptible—effort to press out a moral meaning in this, as she had easily extricated a cosmological meaning in the other tale.

Perhaps we have said too much to introduce these two little unpretending poetical dramas. They might indeed have been allowed to speak for themselves. A new frame often makes a new face; and some of the best known and most exquisite of Shelley's lyrics, when restored to the surroundings for which the poet intended them, needed no other set-off to appeal to the reader with a fresh charm of quiet classical grace and beauty. But the charm will operate all the more unfailingly, if we remember that this clear classical mood was by no means such a common element in the literary atmosphere of the times—not even a permanent element in the authors' lives. We have here none of the feverish ecstasy that lifts Prometheus and Hellas far above the ordinary range of philosophical or political poetry. But Shelley's encouragement, probably his guidance and supervision, have raised his wife's inspiration to a place considerably higher than that of Frankenstein or Valperga. With all their faults these pages reflect some of that irradiation which Shelley cast around his own life—the irradiation of a dream beauteous and generous, beauteous in its theology (or its substitute for theology) and generous even in its satire of human weaknesses.

Footnotes

1 Essay on the Study of Literature, § 56.
2 Blake, Poetical Sketches, 1783.
3 Modern Painters, iii. 317
4 Sonnet 'The world is too much with us'; cf. The Excursion, iv. 851-57.
5 The Piccolomini, II, iv.
6 At least as far as England is concerned. For France, cf. Canat, a renaissance de la Grèce antique, Hachette, Paris, 1911.
7 J. A, Symonds, Studies of the Greek Poets, ii, p. 258.
8 As pointed out by Brunetière, Évolution de la Poésie lyrique, ii, p. 147.
9 Edinb. Rev., July 1808.
10 Cf. our Shelley's Prose in the Bodleian MSS., 1910, p. 124.
11 From the 'Boscombe' MSS. Unpublished.
12 Josh. iv. 8.—These notes are *not* Shelley's.
13 Theogn. 5 foll.; Homer's Hymn to Apollo, i. 25.
14 Probably Xenophon, Cyrop. VIII. vii. 2.
15 Gen. vi.
16 Iliad, xxiv.
17 Shelley may refer to the proverbial phrase 'to kick against the pricks' (Acts xxvi. 14), which, however, is found in Pindar and Euripides as well as in Aeschylus (Prom. 323).
18 Trelawny's letter, 3 April 1870; in Mr. H. Buxton Forman's edition, 1910, p. 229.
19 I. e. ed. H. Buxton Forman, p. 253.
20 Demeter and Persephone, 1889; The Garden of Proserpine, 1866; The Appeasement of Demeter, 1888.
21 To adduce an example—in what is probably not an easily accessible book to-day: Proserpine, distributing her flowers, thus addresses one of her nymphs:
　　For this lily,
Where can it hang but at Cyane's breast!
And yet 'twill wither on so white a bed,
If flowers have sense for envy.
22 There is one by poor Christopher Smart.
23 Perhaps her somewhat wearying second act, on the effects of the

gold-transmuting gift, would have been shorter, if Ovid (Metam. xi. 108-30) had not himself gone into such details on the subject.

MYTHOLOGICAL DRAMAS.

Unless otherwise pointed out—by brackets, or in the notes—the text, spelling, and punctuation of the MS. have been strictly adhered to.

PROSERPINE.

A DRAMA IN TWO ACTS.

DRAMATIS PERSONAE

Ceres.
Proserpine.
Ino, Eunoe Nymphs attendant upon Proserpine.
Iris.
Arethusa, Naiad of a Spring.

Shades from Hell, among which Ascalaphus.

Scene; the plain of Enna, in Sicily.

PROSERPINE.

ACT I.

Scene; a beautiful plain, shadowed on one side by an overhanging rock, on the other a chesnut wood. Etna at a distance.

Enter Ceres, Proserpine, Ino and Eunoe.

Pros. Dear Mother, leave me not! I love to rest
Under the shadow of that hanging cave
And listen to your tales. Your Proserpine
Entreats you stay; sit on this shady bank,
And as I twine a wreathe tell once again
The combat of the Titans and the Gods;
Or how the Python fell beneath the dart
Of dread Apollo; or of Daphne's change,—
That coyest Grecian maid, whose pointed leaves
Now shade her lover's brow. And I the while
Gathering the starry flowers of this fair plain
Will weave a chaplet, Mother, for thy hair.
But without thee, the plain I think is vacant,
Its[1] blossoms fade,—its tall fresh grasses droop,
Nodding their heads like dull things half asleep;—
Go not, dear Mother, from your Proserpine.

[2]

Cer. My lovely child, it is high Jove's command:—
The golden self-moved seats surround his throne,
The nectar is poured out by Ganymede,
And the ambrosia fills the golden baskets;
They drink, for Bacchus is already there,
But none will eat till I dispense the food.
I must away—dear Proserpine, farewel!—
Eunoe can tell thee how the giants fell;
Or dark-eyed Ino sing the saddest change
Of Syrinx or of Daphne, or the doom
Of impious Prometheus, and the boy
Of fair Pandora, Mother of mankind.
This only charge I leave thee and thy nymphs,—
Depart not from each other; be thou circled
By that fair guard, and then no earth-born Power
Would tempt my wrath, and steal thee from their sight[.]
But wandering alone, by feint or force,
You might be lost, and I might never know

Thy hapless fate. Farewel, sweet daughter mine,
Remember my commands.

Pros. —Mother, farewel!
Climb the bright sky with rapid wings; and swift
As a beam shot from great Apollo's bow
Rebounds from the calm mirror of the sea
Back to his quiver in the Sun, do thou
Return again to thy loved Proserpine.

(Exit Ceres.)

[3]

And now, dear Nymphs, while the hot sun is high
Darting his influence right upon the plain,
Let us all sit beneath the narrow shade
That noontide Etna casts.—And, Ino, sweet,
Come hither; and while idling thus we rest,
Repeat in verses sweet the tale which says
How great Prometheus from Apollo's car
Stole heaven's fire—a God-like gift for Man!
Or the more pleasing tale of Aphrodite;
How she arose from the salt Ocean's foam,
And sailing in her pearly shell, arrived
On Cyprus sunny shore, where myrtles[2] bloomed
And sweetest flowers, to welcome Beauty's Queen;
And ready harnessed on the golden sands
Stood milk-white doves linked to a sea-shell car,
With which she scaled the heavens, and took her seat
Among the admiring Gods.

Eun. Proserpine's tale
Is sweeter far than Ino's sweetest aong.

Pros. Ino, you knew erewhile a River-God,
Who loved you well and did you oft entice
To his transparent waves and flower-strewn banks.
He loved high poesy and wove sweet sounds,

And would sing to you as you sat reclined
On the fresh grass beside his shady cave,
From which clear waters bubbled, dancing forth,

|4|

And spreading freshness in the noontide air.
When you returned you would enchant our ears
With tales and songs which did entice the fauns,[3]
With Pan their King from their green haunts, to hear.
Tell me one now, for like the God himself,
Tender they were and fanciful, and wrapt
The hearer in sweet dreams of shady groves,
Blue skies, and clearest, pebble-paved streams.

Ino. I will repeat the tale which most I loved;
Which tells how lily-crowned Arethusa,
Your favourite Nymph, quitted her native Greece,
Flying the liquid God Alpheus, who followed,
Cleaving the desarts of the pathless deep,
And rose in Sicily, where now she flows
The clearest spring of Enna's gifted plain.

(By Shelley)[4]

  Arethusa arose
  From her couch of snows,
 In the Acroceraunian mountains,—
  From cloud, and from crag,
  With many a jag,
 Shepherding her bright fountains.
  She leapt down the rocks
  With her rainbow locks,
 Streaming among the streams,—

|5|

  Her steps paved with green
  The downward ravine,

Which slopes to the Western gleams: —
    And gliding and springing,
    She went, ever singing
In murmurs as soft as sleep;
    The Earth seemed to love her
    And Heaven smiled above her,
As she lingered towards the deep.

    Then Alpheus bold
    On his glacier cold,
With his trident the mountains strook;
    And opened a chasm
    In the rocks; — with the spasm
All Erymanthus shook.
    And the black south wind
    It unsealed behind
The urns of the silent snow,
    And earthquake and thunder
    Did rend in sunder
The bars of the springs below: —
    And the beard and the hair
    Of the river God were
Seen through the torrent's sweep

[6]

    As he followed the light
    Of the fleet nymph's flight
To the brink of the Dorian deep.

    Oh, save me! oh, guide me!
    And bid the deep hide me,
For he grasps me now by the hair!
    The loud ocean heard,
    To its blue depth stirred,
And divided at her prayer[,]
    And under the water
    The Earth's white daughter

Fled like a sunny beam,
   Behind her descended
   Her billows unblended
With the brackish Dorian stream:—
   Like a gloomy stain
   On the Emerald main
Alpheus rushed behind,
   As an eagle pursueing
   A dove to its ruin,
Down the streams of the cloudy wind.

[7]

   Under the bowers
   Where the Ocean Powers
Sit on their pearled thrones,
   Through the coral woods
   Of the weltering floods,
Over heaps of unvalued stones;
   Through the dim beams,
   Which amid the streams
Weave a network of coloured light,
   And under the caves,
   Where the shadowy waves
Are as green as the forest's5 night:—
   Outspeeding the shark,
   And the sword fish dark,
Under the Ocean foam,6
   And up through the rifts
   Of the mountain clifts,
They passed to their Dorian Home.

   And now from their fountains
   In Enna's mountains,
Down one vale where the morning basks,

    Like friends once parted,
    Grown single hearted
They ply their watery tasks.

[8]

    At sunrise they leap
    From their cradles steep
In the cave of the shelving hill[,—]
    At noontide they flow
    Through the woods below
And the meadows of asphodel,—
    And at night they sleep
    In the rocking deep
Beneath the Ortygian shore;—
    Like spirits that lie
    In the azure sky,
When they love, but live no more.

Pros. Thanks, Ino dear, you have beguiled an hour
With poesy that might make pause to list
The nightingale in her sweet evening song.
But now no more of ease and idleness,
The sun stoops to the west, and Enna's plain
Is overshadowed by the growing form
Of giant Etna:—Nymphs, let us arise,
And cull the sweetest flowers of the field,
And with swift fingers twine a blooming wreathe
For my dear Mother's rich and waving hair.

Eunoe. Violets blue and white anemonies

[9]

Bloom on the plain,—but I will climb the brow
Of that o'erhanging hill, to gather thence

That loveliest rose, it will adorn thy crown;
Ino, guard Proserpine till my return.

(Exit.)

Ino. How lovely is this plain!—Nor Grecian vale,
Nor bright Ausonia's ilex bearing shores,
The myrtle bowers of Aphrodite's sweet isle,
Or Naxos burthened with the luscious vine,
Can boast such fertile or such verdant fields
As these, which young Spring sprinkles with her stars;—
Nor Crete which boasts fair Amalthea's horn
Can be compared with the bright golden7 fields
Of Ceres, Queen of plenteous Sicily.

Pros. Sweet Ino, well I know the love you bear
My dearest Mother prompts your partial voice,
And that love makes you doubly dear to me.
But you are idling,—look[,] my lap is full
Of sweetest flowers;—haste to gather more,
That before sunset we may make our crown.
Last night as we strayed through that glade, methought
The wind that swept my cheek bore on its wings
The scent of fragrant violets, hid
Beneath the straggling underwood; Haste, sweet,
To gather them; fear not—I will not stray.

Ino. Nor fear that I shall loiter in my task.

(Exit.)

[10]

(By Shelley.)

Pros. *(sings as she gathers her flowers.)*
   Sacred Goddess, Mother Earth,
     Thou from whose immortal bosom
   Gods, and men, and beasts have birth,

     Leaf, and blade, and bud, and blossom,
Breathe thine influence most divine
On thine own child Proserpine.

  If with mists of evening dew
    Thou dost nourish these young flowers
  Till they grow in scent and hue
    Fairest children of the hours[,]
  Breathe thine influence most divine
On thine own child Proserpine.

(she looks around.)

My nymphs have left me, neglecting the commands
Of my dear Mother. Where can they have strayed?
Her caution makes me fear to be alone;—
I'll pass that yawning cave and seek the spring
Of Arethuse, where water-lilies bloom
Perhaps the nymph now wakes tending her waves,
She loves me well and oft desires my stay,—

[11]

The lilies shall adorn my mother's crown.

(Exit.)

(After a pause enter Eunoe.)

Eun. I've won my prize! look at this fragrant rose!
But where is Proserpine? Ino has strayed
Too far I fear, and she will be fatigued,
As I am now, by my long toilsome search.

Enter Ino.

Oh! you here, Wanderer! Where is Proserpine?

Ino. My lap's heaped up with sweets; dear Proserpine,
You will not chide me now for idleness;—

Look here are all the treasures of the field,—
First these fresh violets, which crouched beneath
A mossy rock, playing at hide and seek
With both the sight and sense through the high fern;
Star-eyed narcissi & the drooping bells
Of hyacinths; and purple polianthus,
Delightful flowers are these; but where is she,
The loveliest of them all, our Mistress dear?

Eun. I know not, even now I left her here,
Guarded by you, oh Ino, while I climbed
Up yonder steep for this most worthless rose:—
Know you not where she is? Did you forget
Ceres' behest, and thus forsake her child?

Ino. Chide not, unkind Eunoe, I but went

[128]

Down that dark glade, where underneath the shade
Of those high trees the sweetest violets grow,—
I went at her command. Alas! Alas!
My heart sinks down; I dread she may be lost;—
Eunoe, climb the hill, search that ravine,
Whose close, dark sides may hide her from our view:—
Oh, dearest, haste! Is that her snow-white robe?

Eun. No;—'tis a faun9 beside its sleeping Mother,
Browsing the grass;—what will thy Mother say,
Dear Proserpine, what will bright Ceres feel,
If her return be welcomed not by thee?

Ino. These are wild thoughts,—& we are wrong to fear
That any ill can touch the child of heaven;
She is not lost,—trust me, she has but strayed
Up some steep mountain path, or in yon dell,
Or to the rock where yellow wall-flowers grow,
Scaling with venturous step the narrow path

Which the goats fear to tread;—she will return
And mock our fears.

Eun. The sun now dips his beams
In the bright sea; Ceres descends at eve
From Jove's high conclave; if her much-loved child
Should meet her not in yonder golden field,
Where to the evening wind the ripe grain waves

|13|

Its yellow head, how will her heart misgive.
Let us adjure the Naiad of yon brook[,]
She may perchance have seen our Proserpine,
And tell us to what distant field she's strayed:—
Wait thou, dear Ino, here, while I repair
To the tree-shaded source of her swift stream.

(Exit Eunoe.)

Ino. Why does my heart misgive? & scalding tears,
That should but mourn, now prophecy her loss?
Oh, Proserpine! Where'er your luckless fate
Has hurried you,—to wastes of desart sand,
Or black Cymmerian cave, or dread Hell,
Yet Ino still will follow! Look where Eunoe
Comes, with down cast eyes and faltering steps,
I fear the worst;—

Re-enter Eunoe.

Has she not then been seen?

Eun. Alas, all hope is vanished! Hymera says
She slept the livelong day while the hot beams
Of Phoebus drank her waves;—nor did she wake
Until her reed-crowned head was wet with dew;—
If she had passed her grot she slept the while.

Ino. Alas! Alas! I see the golden car,
And hear the flapping of the dragons wings,
Ceres descends to Earth. I dare not stay,
I dare not meet the sorrow of her look[,]

[14]

The angry glance of her severest eyes.

Eun. Quick up the mountain! I will search the dell,
She must return, or I will never more.

(Exit.)

Ino. And yet I will not fly, though I fear much
Her angry frown and just reproach, yet shame
Shall quell this childish fear, all hope of safety
For her lost child rests but in her high power,
And yet I tremble as I see her come.

Enter Ceres.

Cer. Where is my daughter? have I aught to dread?
Where does she stray? Ino, you answer not;—
She was aye wont to meet me in yon field,—
Your looks bode ill;—I fear my child is lost.

Ino. Eunoe now seeks her track among the woods;
Fear not, great Ceres, she has only strayed.

Cer. Alas! My boding heart,—I dread the worst.
Oh, careless nymphs! oh, heedless Proserpine!
And did you leave her wandering by herself?
She is immortal,—yet unusual fear
Runs through my veins. Let all the woods be sought,
Let every dryad, every gamesome faun 10
Tell where they last beheld her snowy feet
Tread the soft, mossy paths of the wild wood.

But that I see the base of Etna firm
I well might fear that she had fallen a prey

[15]

To Earth-born Typheus, who might have arisen
And seized her as the fairest child of heaven,
That in his dreary caverns she lies bound;
It is not so: all is as safe and calm
As when I left my child. Oh, fatal day!
Eunoe does not return: in vain she seeks
Through the black woods and down the darksome glades,
And night is hiding all things from our view.
I will away, and on the highest top
Of snowy Etna, kindle two clear flames.
Night shall not hide her from my anxious search,
No moment will I rest, or sleep, or pause
Till she returns, until I clasp again
My only loved one, my lost Proserpine.

END OF ACT FIRST.

Footnotes

[1] There is an apostrophe *on* the s.
[2] MS. *mytles*.
[3] MS. *fawns*
[4] Inserted in a later hand, here as p. 18.
[5] The intended place of the apostrophe is not clear.
[6] MS. *Ocean' foam* as if a genitive was meant; but cf. *Ocean foam* in the Song of Apollo (Midas).
[7] MS. *the bright gold fields*.
[8] MS. pages numbered 11, 12, &c., to the end instead of 12, 13, &c.
[9] MS. *fawn*.
[10] MS. *fawn*.

ACT II

Scene.
The Plain of Enna as before.
Enter Ino & Eunoe.

Eun. How weary am I! and the hot sun flushes
My cheeks that else were white with fear and grief[.]
E'er since that fatal day, dear sister nymph,
On which we lost our lovely Proserpine,
I have but wept and watched the livelong night
And all the day have wandered through the woods[.]

Ino. How all is changed since that unhappy eve!
Ceres forever weeps, seeking her child,
And in her rage has struck the land with blight;
Trinacria mourns with her;—its fertile fields
Are dry and barren, and all little brooks
Struggling scarce creep within their altered banks;
The flowers that erst were wont with bended heads,
To gaze within the clear and glassy wave,
Have died, unwatered by the failing stream.—
And yet their hue but mocks the deeper grief
Which is the fountain of these bitter tears.
But who is this, that with such eager looks

[17]

Hastens this way?—

Eun. 'Tis fairest Arethuse,
A stranger naiad, yet you know her well.

Ino. My eyes were blind with tears.

Enter Arethusa.

Dear Arethuse,
Methinks I read glad tidings in your eyes,

Your smiles are the swift messengers that bear
A tale of coming joy, which we, alas!
Can answer but with tears, unless you bring
To our grief solace, Hope to our Despair.
Have you found Proserpine? or know you where
The loved nymph wanders, hidden from our search?

Areth. Where is corn-crowned Ceres? I have hastened
To ease her anxious heart.

Eun. Oh! dearest Naiad,
Herald of joy! Now will great Ceres bless
Thy welcome coming & more welcome tale.

Ino. Since that unhappy day when Ceres lost
Her much-loved child, she wanders through the isle;
Dark blight is showered from her looks of sorrow;—
And where tall corn and all seed-bearing grass
Rose from beneath her step, they wither now

[18]

Fading under the frown of her bent brows:
The springs decrease;—the fields whose delicate green
Was late her chief delight, now please alone,
Because they, withered, seem to share her grief.

Areth. Unhappy Goddess! how I pity thee!

Ino. At night upon high Etna's topmost peak
She lights two flames, that shining through the isle
Leave dark no wood, or cave, or mountain path,
Their sunlike splendour makes the moon-beams dim,
And the bright stars are lost within their day.
She's in yon field,—she comes towards this plain,
Her loosened hair has fallen on her neck,
Uncircled by the coronal of grain:—
Her cheeks are wan,—her step is faint & slow.

Enter Ceres.

Cer. I faint with weariness: a dreadful thirst
Possesses me! Must I give up the search?
Oh! never, dearest Proserpine, until
I once more clasp thee in my vacant arms!
Help me, dear Arethuse! fill some deep shell
With the clear waters of thine ice-cold spring,
And bring it me;—I faint with heat and thirst.

Areth. My words are better than my freshest waves[:]

[19]

I saw your Proserpine—

Cer. Arethusa, where?
Tell me! my heart beats quick, & hope and fear
Cause my weak limbs to fail me.—

Areth. Sit, Goddess,
Upon this mossy bank, beneath the shade
Of this tall rock, and I will tell my tale.
The day you lost your child, I left my source.
With my Alpheus I had wandered down
The sloping shore into the sunbright sea;
And at the coast we paused, watching the waves
Of our mixed waters dance into the main:—
When suddenly I heard the thundering tread
Of iron hoofed steeds trampling the ground,
And a faint shriek that made my blood run cold.
I saw the King of Hell in his black car,
And in his arms he bore your fairest child,
Fair as the moon encircled by the night,—
But that she strove, and cast her arms aloft,
And cried, "My Mother!"—When she saw me near
She would have sprung from his detested arms,
And with a tone of deepest grief, she cried,
"Oh, Arethuse!" I hastened at her call—

But Pluto when he saw that aid was nigh,
Struck furiously the green earth with his spear,

[20]

Which yawned,—and down the deep Tartarian gulph
His black car rolled—the green earth closed above.

Cer. (*starting up*)
Is this thy doom, great Jove? & shall Hell's king
Quitting dark Tartarus, spread grief and tears
Among the dwellers of your bright abodes?
Then let him seize the earth itself, the stars,—
And all your wide dominion be his prey!—
Your sister calls upon your love, great King!
As you are God I do demand your help!—
Restore my child, or let all heaven sink,
And the fair world be chaos once again!

Ino. Look[!] in the East that loveliest bow is formed[;]
Heaven's single-arched bridge, it touches now
The Earth, and 'mid the pathless wastes of heaven
It paves a way for Jove's fair Messenger;—
Iris descends, and towards this field she comes.

Areth. Sovereign of Harvests, 'tis the Messenger
That will bring joy to thee. Thine eyes light up
With sparkling hope, thy cheeks are pale with dread.

Enter Iris.

Cer. Speak, heavenly Iris! let thy words be poured
Into my drooping soul, like dews of eve
On a too long parched field.—Where is my Proserpine?

[21]

Iris. Sister of Heaven, as by Joves throne I stood
The voice of thy deep prayer arose,—it filled

The heavenly courts with sorrow and dismay:
The Thunderer frowned, & heaven shook with dread
I bear his will to thee, 'tis fixed by fate,
Nor prayer nor murmur e'er can alter it.
If Proserpine while she has lived in hell
Has not polluted by Tartarian food
Her heavenly essence, then she may return,
And wander without fear on Enna's plain,
Or take her seat among the Gods above.
If she has touched the fruits of Erebus,
She never may return to upper air,
But doomed to dwell amidst the shades of death,
The wife of Pluto and the Queen of Hell.

Cer. Joy treads upon the sluggish heels of care!
The child of heaven disdains Tartarian food.
Pluto[,] give up thy prey! restore my child!

Iris. Soon she will see again the sun of Heaven,
By gloomy shapes, inhabitants of Hell,
Attended, and again behold the field
Of Enna, the fair flowers & the streams,
Her late delight,—& more than all, her Mother.

Ino. Our much-loved, long-lost Mistress, do you come?

[22]

And shall once more your nymphs attend your steps?
Will you again irradiate this isle—
That drooped when you were lost?1 & once again
Trinacria smile beneath your Mother's eye?

(Ceres and her companions are ranged on one side in eager expectation; from, the cave on the other, enter Proserpine, attended by various dark & gloomy shapes bearing torches; among which Ascalaphus. Ceres & Proserpine embrace;—her nymphs surround her.)

Cer. Welcome, dear Proserpine! Welcome to light,
To this green earth and to your Mother's arms.
You are too beautiful for Pluto's Queen;
In the dark Stygian air your blooming cheeks
Have lost their roseate tint, and your bright form
Has faded in that night unfit for thee.

Pros. Then I again behold thee, Mother dear:—
Again I tread the flowery plain of Enna,
And clasp thee, Arethuse, & you, my nymphs;
I have escaped from hateful Tartarus,
The abode of furies and all loathed shapes
That thronged around me, making hell more black.
Oh! I could worship thee, light giving Sun,
Who spreadest warmth and radiance o'er the world.
Look at2 the branches of those chesnut trees,
That wave to the soft breezes, while their stems

[23]

Are tinged with red by the sun's slanting rays.
And the soft clouds that float 'twixt earth and sky.
How sweet are all these sights! There all is night!
No God like that (*pointing to the sun*)
smiles on the Elysian plains,
The air [is] windless, and all shapes are still.

Iris. And must I interpose in this deep joy,
And sternly cloud your hopes? Oh! answer me,
Art thou still, Proserpine, a child of light?
Or hast thou dimmed thy attributes of Heaven
By such Tartarian food as must for ever
Condemn thee to be Queen of Hell & Night?

Pros. No, Iris, no,—I still am pure as thee:
Offspring of light and air, I have no stain
Of Hell. I am for ever thine, oh, Mother!

Cer. (*to the shades from Hell*)
Begone, foul visitants to upper air!
Back to your dens! nor stain the sunny earth
By shadows thrown from forms so foul—Crouch in!
Proserpine, child of light, is not your Queen!

(to the nymphs)

Quick bring my car,—we will ascend to heaven,
Deserting Earth, till by decree of Jove,
Eternal laws shall bind the King of Hell
To leave in peace the offspring of the sky.

Ascal. Stay, Ceres! By the dread decree of Jove

[24]

Your child is doomed to be eternal Queen
Of Tartarus,—nor may she dare ascend
The sunbright regions of Olympian Jove,
Or tread the green Earth 'mid attendant nymphs.
Proserpine, call to mind your walk last eve,
When as you wandered in Elysian groves,
Through bowers for ever green, and mossy walks,
Where flowers never die, nor wind disturbs
The sacred calm, whose silence soothes the dead,
Nor interposing clouds, with dun wings, dim
Its mild and silver light, you plucked its fruit,
You ate of a pomegranate's seeds—

Cer. Be silent,
Prophet of evil, hateful to the Gods!
Sweet Proserpine, my child, look upon me.
You shrink; your trembling form & pallid cheeks
Would make his words seem true which are most false[.]
Thou didst not taste the food of Erebus;—
Offspring of Gods art thou,—nor Hell, nor Jove
Shall tear thee from thy Mother's clasping arms.

Pros. If fate decrees, can we resist? farewel!
Oh! Mother, dearer to your child than light,

[25]

Than all the forms of this sweet earth & sky,
Though dear are these, and dear are my poor nymphs,
Whom I must leave;—oh! can immortals weep?
And can a Goddess die as mortals do,
Or live & reign where it is death to be?
Ino, dear Arethuse, again you lose
Your hapless Proserpine, lost to herself
When she quits you for gloomy Tartarus.

Cer. Is there no help, great Jove? If she depart
I will descend with her—the Earth shall lose
Its proud fertility, and Erebus
Shall bear my gifts throughout th' unchanging year.
Valued till now by thee, tyrant of Gods!
My harvests ripening by Tartarian fires
Shall feed the dead with Heaven's ambrosial food.
Wilt thou not then repent, brother unkind,
Viewing the barren earth with vain regret,
Thou didst not shew more mercy to my child?

Ino. We will all leave the light and go with thee,
In Hell thou shalt be girt by Heaven-born nymphs,
Elysium shall be Enna,—thou'lt not mourn
Thy natal plain, which will have lost its worth
Having lost thee, its nursling and its Queen.

Areth. I will sink down with thee;—my lily crown

[26]

Shall bloom in Erebus, portentous loss
To Earth, which by degrees will fade & fall
In envy of our happier lot in Hell;—

And the bright sun and the fresh winds of heaven
Shall light its depths and fan its stagnant air.

(They cling round Proserpine; the Shades of Hell seperate
and stand between them.)

Ascal. Depart! She is our Queen! Ye may not come!
Hark to Jove's thunder! shrink away in fear
From unknown forms, whose tyranny ye'll feel
In groans and tears if ye insult their power.

Iris. Behold Jove's balance hung in upper sky;
There are ye weighed,—to that ye must submit.

Cer. Oh! Jove, have mercy on a Mother's prayer!
Shall it be nought to be akin to thee?
And shall thy sister, Queen of fertile Earth,
Derided be by these foul shapes of Hell?
Look at the scales, they're poized with equal weights!
What can this mean? Leave me not[,] Proserpine[,]
Cling to thy Mother's side! He shall not dare
Divide the sucker from the parent stem.

(embraces her)

|27|

Ascal. He is almighty! who shall set the bounds
To his high will? let him decide our plea!
Fate is with us, & Proserpine is ours!

(He endeavours to part Ceres & Proserpine, the nymphs
prevent him.)

Cer. Peace, ominous bird of Hell & Night! Depart!
Nor with thy skriech disturb a Mother's grief,
Avaunt! It is to Jove we pray, not thee.

Iris. Thy fate, sweet Proserpine, is sealed by Jove,
When Enna is starred by flowers, and the sun

Shoots his hot rays strait on the gladsome land,
When Summer reigns, then thou shalt live on Earth,
And tread these plains, or sporting with your nymphs,
Or at your Mother's side, in peaceful joy.
But when hard frost congeals the bare, black ground,
The trees have lost their leaves, & painted birds
Wailing for food sail through the piercing air;
Then you descend to deepest night and reign
Great Queen of Tartarus, 'mid3 shadows dire,
Offspring of Hell,—or in the silent groves
Of, fair Elysium through which Lethe runs,
The sleepy river; where the windless air
Is never struck by flight or song of bird,—

[28]

But all is calm and clear, bestowing rest,
After the toil of life, to wretched men,
Whom thus the Gods reward for sufferings
Gods cannot know; a throng of empty shades!
The endless circle of the year will bring
Joy in its turn, and seperation sad;
Six months to light and Earth,—six months to Hell.

Pros. Dear Mother, let me kiss that tear which steals
Down your pale cheek altered by care and grief.
This is not misery; 'tis but a slight change
Prom our late happy lot. Six months with thee,
Each moment freighted with an age of love:
And the six short months in saddest Tartarus
Shall pass in dreams of swift returning joy.
Six months together we shall dwell on earth,
Six months in dreams we shall companions be,
Jove's doom is void; we are forever joined.

Cer. Oh, fairest child! sweet summer visitor!
Thy looks cheer me, so shall they cheer this land
Which I will fly, thou gone. Nor seed of grass,

44

Or corn shall grow, thou absent from the earth;
But all shall lie beneath in hateful night

[29]

Until at thy return, the fresh green springs,
The fields are covered o'er with summer plants.
And when thou goest the heavy grain will droop
And die under my frown, scattering the seeds,
That will not reappear till your return.
Farewel, sweet child, Queen of the nether world,
There shine as chaste Diana's silver car
Islanded in the deep circumfluous night.
Giver of fruits! for such thou shalt be styled,
Sweet Prophetess of Summer, coming forth
From the slant shadow of the wintry earth,
In thy car drawn by snowy-breasted swallows!
Another kiss, & then again farewel!
Winter in losing thee has lost its all,
And will be doubly bare, & hoar, & drear,
Its bleak winds whistling o'er the cold pinched ground
Which neither flower or grass will decorate.
And as my tears fall first, so shall the trees
Shed their changed leaves upon your six months tomb:
The clouded air will hide from Phoebus' eye
The dreadful change your absence operates.
Thus has black Pluto changed the reign of Jove,
He seizes half the Earth when he takes thee.

THE END

Footnotes

1 MS. *this isle?—That drooped when you were lost*
2 MS. Look at—the branches.
3 MS. *mid*

MIDAS.

A DRAMA IN TWO ACTS.

DRAMATIS PERSONAE

Immortals.
Apollo.
Bacchus.
Pan.
Silenus.
Tmolus, God of a Hill.
Fauns, &c.

Mortals.
Midas, King of Phrygia.
Zopyrion, his Prime-Minister.
Asphalion, Lacon, Courtiers.
Courtiers, Attendants, Priests, &c.

Scene, Phrygia.

MIDAS.

ACT I.

Scene; a rural spot; on one side, a bare Hill, on the other an Ilex wood; a stream with reeds on its banks.

The Curtain rises and discovers Tmolus seated on a throne of turf, on his right hand Apollo with his lyre, attended by the Muses; on the left, Pan, fauns, &c.

Enter Midas and Zopyrion.

Midas. The Hours have oped the palace of the dawn
And through the Eastern gates of Heaven, Aurora

Comes charioted on light, her wind-swift steeds,
Winged with roseate clouds, strain up the steep.
She loosely holds the reins, her golden hair,
Its strings outspread by the sweet morning breeze[,]
Blinds the pale stars. Our rural tasks begin;
The young lambs bleat pent up within the fold,
The herds low in their stalls, & the blithe cock
Halloos most loudly to his distant mates.
But who are these we see? these are not men,
Divine of form & sple[n]didly arrayed,

[36]

They sit in solemn conclave. Is that Pan,
Our Country God, surrounded by his Fauns?
And who is he whose crown of gold & harp
Are attributes of high Apollo?

Zopyr. Best
Your majesty retire; we may offend.

Midas. Aye, and at the base thought the coward blood
Deserts your trembling lips; but follow me.
Oh Gods! for such your bearing is, & sure
No mortal ever yet possessed the gold
That glitters on your silken robes; may one,
Who, though a king, can boast of no descent
More noble than Deucalion's stone-formed men[,]
May I demand the cause for which you deign
To print upon this worthless Phrygian earth
The vestige of your gold-inwoven sandals,
Or why that old white-headed man sits there
Upon that grassy throne, & looks as he
Were stationed umpire to some weighty cause[?]

Tmolus. God Pan with his blithe pipe which the Fauns love
Has challenged Phoebus of the golden lyre[,]
Saying his Syrinx can give sweeter notes

Than the stringed instrument Apollo boasts.
I judge between the parties. Welcome, King,

[37]

I am old Tmolus, God of that bare Hill,
You may remain and hear th' Immortals sing.

Mid. [*aside*] My judgement is made up before I hear;
Pan is my guardian God, old-horned Pan,
The Phrygian's God who watches o'er our flocks;
No harmony can equal his blithe pipe.

(Shelley.)

Apollo (sings).

  The sleepless Hours who watch me as I lie,
    Curtained with star-enwoven tapestries,
  From the broad moonlight of the sky,
    Fanning the busy dreams from my dim eyes
  Waken me when their Mother, the grey Dawn,
  Tells them that dreams & that the moon is gone.

  Then I arise, and climbing Heaven's blue dome,
    I walk over the mountains & the waves,
  Leaving my robe upon the Ocean foam,—
    My footsteps pave the clouds with fire; the caves
  Are filled with my bright presence & the air
  Leaves the green Earth to my embraces bare.

  The sunbeams are my shafts with which I kill
    Deceit, that loves the night & fears the day;
  All men who do, or even imagine ill
    Fly me, and from the glory of my ray
  Good minds and open actions take new might
  Until diminished by the reign of night.

[38]

  I feed the clouds, the rainbows & the flowers
     With their etherial colours; the moon's globe
  And the pure stars in their eternal bowers
     Are cinctured with my power as with a robe;
  Whatever lamps on Earth or Heaven may shine
  Are portions of one power, which is mine.

  I stand at noon upon the peak of heaven,
    Then with unwilling steps I wander down
  Into the clouds of the Atlantic even—
    For grief that I depart they weep & frown [;]
  What look is more delightful than the smile
  With which I soothe them from the western isle [?]

  I am the eye with which the Universe
    Beholds itself & knows it is divine.
  All harmony of instrument or verse,
    All prophecy, all medecine is mine;
  All light of art or nature;—to my song
  Victory and praise, in its own right, belong.

(Shelley.)

Pan (sings).

  From the forests and highlands
    We come, we come;
  From the river-girt islands
    W[h]ere loud waves are dumb,
      Listening my sweet pipings;

[39]

  The wind in the reeds & the rushes,
    The bees on the bells of thyme,

The birds on the myrtle bushes[,]
  The cicale above in the lime[,]
And the lizards below in the grass,
Were as silent as ever old Tmolus was
    Listening my sweet pipings.

Liquid Peneus was flowing,
  And all dark Tempe lay
In Pelion's shadow, outgrowing
  The light of the dying day
    Speeded by my sweet pipings.
The Sileni, & Sylvans, & Fauns
  And the nymphs of the woods & the waves
To the edge of the moist river-lawns,
  And the brink of the dewy caves[,]
And all that did then attend & follow
Were silent with love, as you now, Apollo!
    With envy of my sweet pipings.

I sang of the dancing stars,
  I sang of the daedal Earth—-
And of heaven—& the giant wars—
    And Love, & death, [&] birth,

[40]

    And then I changed my pipings,
Singing how down the vale of Menalus,
  I pursued a maiden & clasped a reed,
Gods and men, we are all deluded thus!
  It breaks in our bosom & then we bleed!
All wept, as I think both ye now would
If envy or age had not frozen your blood,
    At the sorrow of my sweet pipings.

Tmol. Phoebus, the palm is thine. The Fauns may dance
To the blithe tune of ever merry Pan;
But wisdom, beauty, & the power divine
Of highest poesy lives within thy strain.
Named by the Gods the King of melody,
Receive from my weak hands a second crown.

Pan. Old Grey-beard, you say false! you think by this
To win Apollo with his sultry beams
To thaw your snowy head, & to renew
The worn out soil of your bare, ugly hill.
I do appeal to Phrygian Midas here;
Let him decide, he is no partial judge.

Mid. Immortal Pan, to my poor, mortal ears
Your sprightly song in melody outweighs
His drowsy tune; he put me fast asleep,
As my prime minister, Zopyrion, knows;

[41]

But your gay notes awoke me, & to you,
If I were Tmolus, would I give the prize.

Apol. And who art thou who dar'st among the Gods
Mingle thy mortal voice? Insensate fool!
Does not the doom of Marsyas fill with dread
Thy impious soul? or would'st thou also be
Another victim to my justest wrath?
But fear no more;—thy punishment shall be
But as a symbol of thy blunted sense.
Have asses' ears! and thus to the whole world
Wear thou the marks of what thou art,
Let Pan himself blush at such a judge.[1]

(Exeunt all except Midas & Zopyrion.)

Mid. What said he? is it true, Zopyrion?
Yet if it be; you must not look on me,

But shut your eyes, nor dare behold my shame.
Ah! here they are! two long, smooth asses['] ears!
They stick upright! Ah, I am sick with shame!

Zopyr. I cannot tell your Majesty my grief,
Or how my soul's oppressed with the sad change
That has, alas! befallen your royal ears.

Mid. A truce to your fine speeches now, Zopyrion;
To you it appertains to find some mode
Of hiding my sad chance, if not you die.

Zopyr. Great King, alas! my thoughts are dull & slow[;]

[42]

Pardon my folly, might they not be cut,
Rounded off handsomely, like human ears [?]

Mid. (*feeling his ears*)
They're long & thick; I fear 'twould give me pain;
And then if vengeful Phoebus should command
Another pair to grow—that will not do.

Zopyr. You wear a little crown of carved gold,
Which just appears to tell you are a king;
If that were large and had a cowl of silk,
Studded with gems, which none would dare gainsay,
Then might you—

Mid. Now you have it! friend,
I will reward you with some princely gift.
But, hark! Zopyrion, not a word of this;
If to a single soul you tell my shame
You die. I'll to the palace the back way
And manufacture my new diadem,
The which all other kings shall imitate
As if they also had my asses['] ears.

(Exit.)

Zopyr. (*watching Midas off*)
He cannot hear me now, and I may laugh!
I should have burst had he staid longer here.
Two long, smooth asses' ears that stick upright;
Oh, that Apollo had but made him bray!
I'll to the palace; there I'll laugh my fill

[43]

With—hold! What were the last words that Midas said?
I may not speak—not to my friends disclose
The strangest tale? ha! ha! and when I laugh
I must not tell the cause? none know the truth?
None know King Midas has—but who comes here?
It is Asphalion: he knows not this change;
I must look grave & sad; for now a smile
If Midas knows it may prove capital.
Yet when I think of those—oh! I shall die,
In either way, by silence or by speech.

Enter Asphalion.

Asphal. Know you, Zopyrion?—

Zopyr. What[!] you know it too?
Then I may laugh;—oh, what relief is this!
How does he look, the courtiers gathering round?
Does he hang down his head, & his ears too?
Oh, I shall die! (*laughs.*)

Asph. He is a queer old dog,
Yet not so laughable. 'Tis true, he's drunk,
And sings and reels under the broad, green leaves,
And hanging clusters of his crown of grapes.—

Zopyr. A crown of grapes! but can that hide his ears[?]

Asph. His ears!—Oh, no! they stick upright between.
When Midas saw him—

Zopyr. Whom then do you mean?

[44]

Did you not say—

Asph. I spoke of old Silenus;
Who having missed his way in these wild woods,
And lost his tipsey company—was found
Sucking the juicy clusters of the vines
That sprung where'er he trod:—and reeling on
Some shepherds found him in yon ilex wood.
They brought him to the king, who honouring him
For Bacchus' sake, has gladly welcomed him,
And will conduct him with solemnity
To the disconsolate Fauns from whom he's strayed.
But have you seen the new-fashioned diadem[2]
That Midas wears?—

Zopyr. Ha! he has got it on!—
Know you the secret cause why with such care
He hides his royal head? you have not seen—

Asph. Seen what?

Zopyr. Ah! then, no matter:— (*turns away agitated*.)
I dare not sneak or stay[;]
If I remain I shall discover all.

Asp. I see the king has trusted to your care
Some great state secret which you fain would hide.
I am your friend, trust my fidelity,

[45]

If you're in doubt I'll be your counsellor.

54

Zopyr. (*with great importance*.)
Secret, Asphalion! How came you to know?
If my great master (which I do not say)
Should think me a fit friend in whom to pour
The weighty secrets of his royal heart,
Shall I betray his trust? It is not so;—
I am a poor despised slave.—No more!
Join we the festal band which will conduct
Silenus to his woods again?

Asph. My friend,
Wherefore mistrust a faithful heart? Confide
The whole to me;—I will be still as death.

Zopyr. As death! you know not what you say; farewell[!]
A little will I commune with my soul,
And then I'll join you at the palace-gate.

Asph. Will you then tell me?—

Zopyr. Cease to vex, my friend,
Your soul and mine with false suspicion, (*aside*) Oh!
I am choked! I'd give full ten years of my life
To tell, to laugh—& yet I dare not speak.

[46]

Asph. Zopyrion, remember that you hurt
The trusting bosom of a faithful friend
By your unjust concealment.

(Exit.)

Zopyr. Oh, he's gone!
To him I dare not speak, nor yet to Lacon;
No human ears may hear what must be told.
I cannot keep it in, assuredly;
I shall some night discuss it in my sleep.
It will not keep! Oh! greenest reeds that sway

And nod your feathered heads beneath the sun,
Be you depositaries of my soul,
Be you my friends in this extremity[:]
I shall not risk my head when I tell you
The fatal truth, the heart oppressing fact,

(*stooping down & whispering*)

(Enter Midas, Silenus & others, who fall back during the scene; Midas is always anxious about his crown, & Zopyrion gets behind him & tries to smother his laughter.)

Silen. (*very drunk*) Again I find you, Bacchus, runaway!
Welcome, my glorious boy! Another time
Stray not; or leave your poor old foster-father
In the wild mazes of a wood, in which
I might have wandered many hundred years,
Had not some merry fellows helped me out,
And had not this king kindly welcomed me,
I might have fared more ill than you erewhile
In Pentheus' prisons, that death fated rogue.

Bac. (*to Midas*.) To you I owe great thanks & will reward
Your hospitality. Tell me your name
And what this country is.

Midas. My name is Midas—

The Reeds (*nodding their heads*).

|49|

Midas, the king, has the ears of an ass.

Midas. (*turning round & seizing Zopyrion*).
Villain, you lie! he dies who shall repeat
Those traitrous words. Seize on Zopyrion!

The Reeds. Midas, the king, has the ears of an ass.

Mid. Search through the crowd; it is a woman's voice
That dares belie her king, & makes her life
A forfeit to his fury.

Asph. There is no woman here.

Bac. Calm yourself, Midas; none believe the tale,
Some impious man or gamesome faun dares feign
In vile contempt of your most royal ears.
Off with your crown, & shew the world the lie!

Mid. (*holding his crown tight*)
Never! What[!] shall a vile calumnious slave
Dictate the actions of a crowned king?
Zopyrion, this lie springs from you—you perish!

Zopy. I, say that Midas has got asses' ears?
May great Apollo strike me with his shaft
If to a single soul I ever told
So false, so foul a calumny!

[50]

Bac. Midas!

The Reeds. Midas, the king, has the ears of an ass.

Bac. Silence! or by my Godhead I strike dead
Who shall again insult the noble king.
Midas, you are my friend, for you have saved
And hospitably welcomed my old faun;
Choose your reward, for here I swear your wish,
Whatever it may be, shall be fulfilled.

Zopyr. (*aside*) Sure he will wish his asses' ears in Styx.

Midas. What[!] may I choose from out the deep, rich mine
Of human fancy, & the wildest thoughts
That passed till now unheeded through my brain,
A wish, a hope, to be fulfilled by you?

Nature shall bend her laws at my command,
And I possess as my reward one thing
That I have longed for with unceasing care.

Bac. Pause, noble king, ere you express this wish[.]
Let not an error or rash folly spoil
My benefaction; pause and then declare,
For what you ask shall be, as I have sworn.

Mid. Let all I touch be gold, most glorious gold!

[51]

Let me be rich! and where I stretch my hands,
(That like Orion I could touch the stars!)
Be radiant gold! God Bacchus, you have sworn,
I claim your word,—my ears are quite forgot!

The Reeds. Midas, the king, has the ears of an ass.

Mid. You lie, & yet I care not—

Zopyr. (*aside to Midas*) Yet might I
But have advised your Majesty, I would
Have made one God undo the other's work—

Midas. (*aside to Zopyr*).
Advise yourself, my friend, or you may grow
Shorter by a head ere night.—I am blessed,
Happier than ever earthly man could boast.
Do you fulfil your words?

Bac. Yes, thoughtless man!
And much I fear if you have not the ears
You have the judgement of an ass. Farewel!
I found you rich & happy; & I leave you,
Though you know it not, miserably poor.
Your boon is granted,—touch! make gold! Some here

Help carry old Silenus off, who sleeps
The divine sleep of heavy wine. Farewel!

Mid. Bacchus, divine, how shall I pay my thanks[?]

(Exeunt.)

END OF FIRST ACT.

Footnotes

[1] A syllable here, a whole foot in the previous line, appear to be missing.
[2] Another halting line. Cf. again, p. [47], l. 3; p. [55], l. 11; p. [59], l.1; p. [61], l. 1; p. [64], l. 14.]

ACT II

Scene; a splendid apartment in the Palace of Midas.

Enter Midas
(with a golden rose in his hand).

Mid. Gold! glorious gold! I am made up of gold!
I pluck a rose, a silly, fading rose,
Its soft, pink petals change to yellow gold;
Its stem, its leaves are gold—and what before
Was fit for a poor peasant's festal dress
May now adorn a Queen. I lift a stone,
A heavy, useless mass, a slave would spurn,
What is more valueless? 'Tis solid gold!
A king might war on me to win the same.
And as I pass my hand thus through the air,
A little shower of sightless dust falls down
A shower of gold. O, now I am a king!
I've spread my hands against my palace walls,
I've set high ladders up, that I may touch
Each crevice and each cornice with my hands,

And it will all be gold:—a golden palace,
Surrounded by a wood of golden trees,
Which will bear golden fruits.—The very ground
My naked foot treads on is yellow gold,

[53]

Invaluable gold! my dress is gold!
Now I am great! Innumerable armies
Wait till my gold collects them round my throne;
I see my standard made of woven gold.
Waving o'er Asia's utmost Citadels,
Guarded by myriads invincible.
Or if the toil of war grows wearisome,
I can buy Empires:—India shall be mine,
Its blooming beauties, gold-encrusted baths,
Its aromatic groves and palaces,
All will be mine! Oh, Midas, ass-eared king!
I love thee more than any words can tell,
That thus thy touch, thou man akin to Gods,
Can change all earth to heaven,—Olympian gold!
For what makes heaven different from earth!
Look how my courtiers come! Magnificent!
None shall dare wait on me but those who bear
An empire on their backs in sheets of gold.
Oh, what a slave I was! my flocks & kine,
My vineyards & my corn were all my wealth
And men esteemed me rich; but now Great Jove
Transcends me but by lightning, and who knows
If my gold win not the Cyclopean Powers,
And Vulcan, who must hate his father's rule,

[54]

To forge me bolts?—and then—but hush! they come.

Enter Zopyrion, Asphalion, & Lacon.

Lac. Pardon us, mighty king—

Mid. What would ye, slaves?
Oh! I could buy you all with one slight touch
Of my gold-making hand!

Asph. Royal Midas,
We humbly would petition for relief.

Mid. Relief I Bring me your copper coin, your brass,
Or what ye will—ye'll speedily be rich.

Zopyr. 'Tis not for gold, but to be rid of gold,
That we intrude upon your Majesty.
I fear that you will suffer by this gift,
As we do now. Look at our backs bent down
With the huge weight of the great cloaks of gold.
Permit us to put on our shabby dress,
Our poor despised garments of light wool:—
We walk as porters underneath a load.
Pity, great king, our human weaknesses,
Nor force us to expire—

Mid. Begone, ye slaves!
Go clothe your wretched limbs in ragged skins!
Take an old carpet to wrap round your legs,

[55]

A broad leaf for your feet—ye shall not wear
That dress—those golden sandals—monarch like.

Asph. If you would have us walk a mile a day
We cannot thus—already we are tired
With the huge weight of soles of solid gold.

Mid. Pitiful wretches! Earth-born, groveling dolts!
Begone! nor dare reply to my just wrath!
Never behold me more! or if you stay
Let not a sigh, a shrug, a stoop betray
What poor, weak, miserable men you are.

Not as I—I am a God! Look, dunce!
I tread or leap beneath this load of gold!

(Jumps & stops suddenly.)

I've hurt my back:—this cloak is wondrous hard!
No more of this! my appetite would say
The hour is come for my noon-day repast.

Lac. It comes borne in by twenty lusty slaves,
Who scarce can lift the mass of solid gold,
That lately was a table of light wood.
Here is the heavy golden ewer & bowl,
In which, before you eat, you wash your hands.

Mid. (*lifting up the ewer*)
This is to be a king! to touch pure gold!

[56]

Would that by touching thee, Zopyrion,
I could transmute thee to a golden man;
A crowd of golden slaves to wait on me!

(Pours the water on his hands.)

But how is this? the water that I touch
Falls down a stream of yellow liquid gold,
And hardens as it falls. I cannot wash—
Pray Bacchus, I may drink! and the soft towel
With which I'd wipe my hands transmutes itself
Into a sheet of heavy gold.—No more!
I'll sit and eat:—I have not tasted food
For many hours, I have been so wrapt
In golden dreams of all that I possess,
I had not time to eat; now hunger calls
And makes me feel, though not remote in power
From the immortal Gods, that I need food,
The only remnant of mortality!

(In vain attempts to eat of several dishes.)

Alas! my fate! 'tis gold! this peach is gold!
This bread, these grapes & all I touch! this meat
Which by its scent quickened my appetite
Has lost its scent, its taste,—'tis useless gold.

Zopyr. (*aside*) He'd better now have followed my advice.

[57]

He starves by gold yet keeps his asses' ears.

Mid. Asphalion, put that apple to my mouth;
If my hands touch it not perhaps I eat.
Alas! I cannot bite! as it approached
I felt its fragrance, thought it would be mine,
But by the touch of my life-killing lips
'Tis changed from a sweet fruit to tasteless gold,
Bacchus will not refresh me by his gifts,
The liquid wine congeals and flies my taste.
Go, miserable slaves! Oh, wretched king!
Away with food! Its sight now makes me sick.
Bring in my couch! I will sleep off my care,
And when I wake I'll coin some remedy.
I dare not bathe this sultry day, for fear
I be enclosed in gold. Begone!
I will to rest:—oh, miserable king!

(Exeunt all but Midas. He lies down, turns restlessly for some time & then rises.)

Oh! fool! to wish to change all things to gold!
Blind Ideot that I was! This bed is gold;
And this hard, weighty pillow, late so soft,
That of itself invited me to rest,
Is a hard lump, that if I sleep and turn

[58]

I may beat out my brains against its sides.
Oh! what a wretched thing I am! how blind!
I cannot eat, for all my food is gold;
Drink flies my parched lips, and my hard couch
Is worse than rock to my poor bruised sides.
I cannot walk; the weight of my gold soles
Pulls me to earth:—my back is broke beneath
These gorgeous garments— (*throws off his cloak*)
Lie there, golden cloak!
There on thy kindred earth, lie there and rot!
I dare not touch my forehead with my palm
For fear my very flesh should turn to gold.
Oh! let me curse thee, vilest, yellow dirt!
Here, on my knees, thy martyr lifts his voice,
A poor, starved wretch who can touch nought but thee[,]
Wilt thou refresh me in the heat of noon?
Canst thou be kindled for me when I'm cold?
May all men, & the immortal Gods,
Hate & spurn thee as wretched I do now.

(Kicks the couch, & tries to throw down the pillow but cannot lift it.)

I'd dash, thee to the earth, but that thy weight

[59]

Preserves thee, abhorred, Tartarian Gold!
Bacchus, O pity, pardon, and restore me!
Who waits?

Enter Lacon.

Go bid the priests that they prepare
Most solemn song and richest sacrifise;—
Which I may not dare touch, lest it should turn
To most unholy gold.

Lacon. Pardon me, oh King,
But perhaps the God may give that you may eat,
And yet your touch be magic.

Mid. No more, thou slave!
Gold is my fear, my bane, my death! I hate
Its yellow glare, its aspect hard and cold.
I would be rid of all.—Go bid them haste.

(Exit Lacon.)

Oh, Bacchus I be propitious to their prayer!
Make me a hind, clothe me in ragged skins—
And let my food be bread, unsavoury roots,
But take from me the frightful curse of gold.
Am I not poor? Alas! how I am changed!
Poorer than meanest slaves, my piles of wealth
Cannot buy for me one poor, wretched dish:—
In summer heat I cannot bathe, nor wear
A linen dress; the heavy, dull, hard metal
Clings to me till I pray for poverty.

|60|

Enter Zopyrion, Asphalion & Lacon.

Zopyr. The sacrifice is made, & the great God,
Pitying your ills, oh King, accepted it,
Whilst his great oracle gave forth these words.
"Let poor king Midas bathe in the clear stream
"Of swift Pactolus, & to those waves tran[s]fer
"The gold-transmuting power, which he repents."

Mid. Oh joy! Oh Bacchus, thanks for this to thee
Will I each year offer three sucking lambs—
Games will I institute—nor Pan himself
Shall have more honour than thy deity.
Haste to the stream,—I long to feel the cool
And liquid touch of its divinest waves.

(Exeunt all except Zopyrion and Asphalion.)

Asph. Off with our golden sandals and our cloaks!
Oh, I shall ever hate the sight of gold!
Poor, wealthy Midas runs as if from death
To rid him quick of this meta[l]lic curse.

Zopyr. (*aside*) I wonder if his asses[']ears are gold;
What would I give to let the secret out?
Gold! that is trash, we have too much of it,—
But I would give ten new born lambs to tell
This most portentous truth—but I must choke.

Asph. Now we shall tend our flocks and reap our corn
As we were wont, and not be killed by gold.

[61]

Golden fleeces threatened our poor sheep,
The very showers as they fell from heaven
Could not refresh the earth; the wind blew gold,
And as we walked[1] the thick sharp-pointed atoms
Wounded our faces—the navies would have sunk—

Zopyr. All strangers would have fled our gold-cursed shore,
Till we had bound our wealthy king, that he
Might leave the green and fertile earth unchanged;—
Then in deep misery he would have shook
His golden chains & starved.

Enter Lacon.

Lacon. Sluggards, how now I
Have you not been to gaze upon the sight?
To see the noble king cast off the gift
Which he erewhile so earnestly did crave[?]

Asph. I am so tired with the weight of gold
I bore to-day I could not budge a foot

To see the finest sight Jove could display.
But tell us, Lacon, what he did and said.

Lac. Although he'd fain have run[,] his golden dress
And heavy sandals made the poor king limp
As leaning upon mine and the high priest's arm,
He hastened to Pactolus. When he saw
The stream—"Thanks to the Gods!" he cried aloud
In joy; then having cast aside his robes
He leaped into the waves, and with his palm

[62]

Throwing the waters high—"This is not gold,"
He cried, "I'm free, I have got rid of gold."
And then he drank, and seizing with delight
A little leaf that floated down the stream,
"Thou art not gold," he said—

Zopyr. But all this time—
Did you behold?—Did he take off his crown?—

Lacon. No:—It was strange to see him as he plunged
Hold tight his crown with his left hand the while.

Zopyr. (*aside*) Alas, my fate! I thought they had been seen.

Lac. He ordered garments to the river side
Of coarsest texture;—those that erst he wore
He would not touch, for they were trimmed with gold.

Zopyr. And yet he did not throw away his crown?

Lac. He ever held it tight as if he thought
Some charm attached to its remaining there.
Perhaps he is right;—know you, Zopyrion,
If that strange voice this morning spoke the truth?

Zopyr. Nay guess;—think of what passed & you can judge.
I dare not—I know nothing of his ears.

Lac. I am resolved some night when he sleeps sound
To get a peep.—No more,'tis he that comes.
He has now lost the boon that Bacchus gave,
Having bestowed it on the limpid waves.

[63]

Now over golden sands Pactolus runs,
And as it flows creates a mine of wealth.

Enter Midas, (with grapes in his hand).

Mid. I see again the trees and smell the flowers
With colours lovelier than the rainbow's self;
I see the gifts of rich-haired Ceres piled
And eat. (*holding up the grapes*)
This is not yellow, dirty gold,
But blooms with precious tints, purple and green.
I hate this palace and its golden floor,
Its cornices and rafters all of gold:—
I'll build a little bower of freshest green,
Canopied o'er with leaves & floored with moss:—
I'll dress in skins;—I'll drink from wooden cups
And eat on wooden platters—sleep on flock;
None but poor men shall dare attend on me.
All that is gold I'll banish from my court,
Gilding shall be high treason to my state,
The very name of gold shall be crime capital[.]

Zopyr. May we not keep our coin?

Mid. No, Zopyrion,
None but the meanest peasants shall have gold.
It is a sordid, base and dirty thing:—
Look at the grass, the sky, the trees, the flowers,

[64]

These are Joves treasures & they are not gold:—
Now they are mine, I am no longer cursed.—
The hapless river hates its golden sands,
As it rolls over them, having my gift;—
Poor harmless shores! they now are dirty gold.
How I detest it! Do not the Gods hate gold?
Nature displays the treasures that she loves,
She hides gold deep in the earth & piles above
Mountains & rocks to keep the monster down.

Asph. They say Apollo's sunny car is gold.

Mid. Aye, so it is for Gold belongs to him:—
But Phoebus is my bitterest enemy,
And what pertains to him he makes my bane.

Zopyr. What [!] will your Majesty tell the world?—

Mid. Peace, vile gossip! Asphalion, come you here.
Look at those golden columns; those inlaid walls;
The ground, the trees, the flowers & precious food
That in my madness I did turn to gold:—
Pull it all down, I hate its sight and touch;
Heap up my cars & waggons with the load
And yoke my kine to drag it to the sea:
Then crowned with flowers, ivy & Bacchic vine,
And singing hymns to the immortal Gods,

[65]

We will ascend ships freighted with the gold,
And where no plummet's line can sound the depth
Of greedy Ocean, we will throw it in,
All, all this frightful heap of yellow dirt.
Down through the dark, blue waters it will sink,
Frightening the green-haired Nereids from their sport
And the strange Tritons—the waves will close above

And I, thank Bacchus, ne'er shall see it more!
And we will make all echoing heaven ring
With our loud hymns of thanks, & joyous pour
Libations in the deep, and reach the land,
Rich, happy, free & great, that we have lost
Man's curse, heart-bartering, soul-enchaining gold.

FINIS.

Footnotes

1 MS. *as he walked.*

Made in United States
Orlando, FL
26 November 2022